Debating
Challenge!

Developing Major Debate Skills

Neill Porteous

1

Table of **Contents**

Features

The Debating Challenge series help English learners to develop key debating skills.

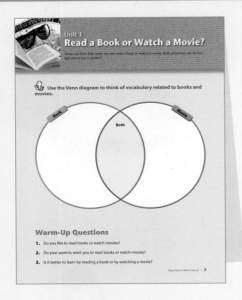

Introduction and Warm-Up Questions

- A variety of activities that introduce each unit's theme to students

- Warm-up questions that allow students to understand major aspects of each unit's theme

Reading

- Carefully chosen debating issues that are relevant to today's teenagers

- Expertly written texts that present different opinions clearly and logically

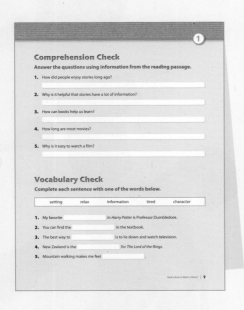

Comprehension Check & Vocabulary Check

- Comprehension questions that help students understand each unit's text

- Vocabulary questions that enable students to learn how to use key words in context

Opinion Practice

- Two different activities that teach learners how to support and refute different opinions

- Various opinions that address major aspects of each unit's debating issue

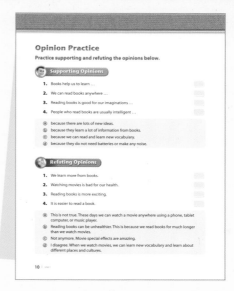

Opinion Examples

- Two different opinions that are based on logical reasoning

- Text analysis activities that reinforce critical reading and thinking skills

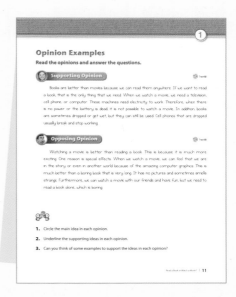

Discussion Questions & Let's Debate

- Discussion questions that are closely associated with each unit's debating issue

- Let's Debate section that invites students to explore and debate major issues

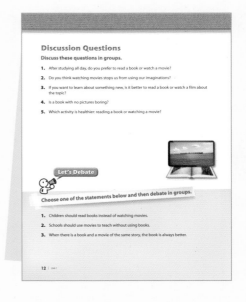

Unit 1
Read a Book or Watch a Movie?

When we have free time, we can read a book or watch a movie. Both activities can be fun, but which one is better?

Use the Venn diagram to think of vocabulary related to books and movies.

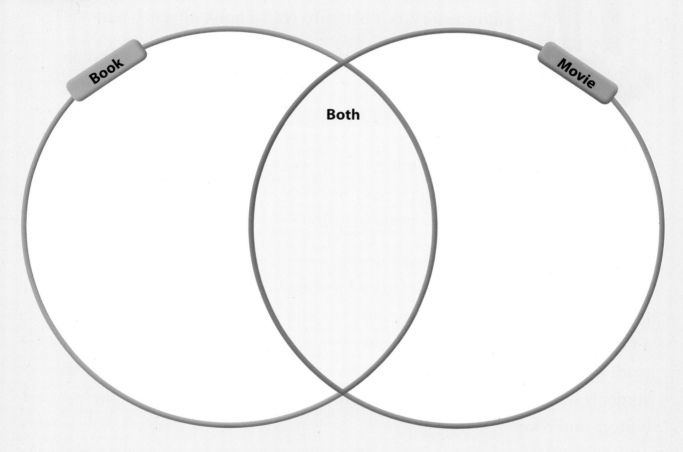

Book   Both   Movie

Warm-Up Questions

1. Do you like to read books or watch movies?

2. Do your parents want you to read books or watch movies?

3. Is it better to learn by reading a book or by watching a movie?

DC1-01
MP3

Read a Book or Watch a Movie?

A long time ago, the only way to enjoy a story was by listening to a storyteller. These days, people can enjoy stories through books and movies. Then, if we want to enjoy a story, is it better to read a book or watch a movie?

Some people believe that it is better to read books. First, books have a lot of information. So, the reader can learn many things about the characters and setting of the story. Next, books help us to learn. When we read, we can improve our reading skills, learn new vocabulary, and learn about good grammar, too. In addition, reading books in a different language is a great way to improve our language ability.

However, other people think that watching a movie is much better. One reason is that movies are quite short. Most films are only around two hours long. People are busy these days, but they often have enough time to enjoy a film. In addition, watching a movie is easy. Students are usually tired after reading books all day, and they don't want to read when they get home. If students watch a movie, all they need to do is sit down, press the "Play" button, and relax.

Comprehension Check

Answer the questions using information from the reading passage.

1. How did people enjoy stories long ago?

2. Why is it helpful that stories have a lot of information?

3. How can books help us learn?

4. How long are most movies?

5. Why is it easy to watch a film?

Vocabulary Check

Complete each sentence with one of the words below.

setting	relax	information	tired	character

1. My favorite _____ in *Harry Potter* is Professor Dumbledore.

2. You can find the _____ in the textbook.

3. The best way to _____ is to lie down and watch television.

4. New Zealand is the _____ for *The Lord of the Rings*.

5. Mountain walking makes me feel _____ .

Opinion Practice

Practice supporting and refuting the opinions below.

 Supporting Opinions

1. Books help us to learn …

2. We can read books anywhere …

3. Reading books is good for our imaginations …

4. People who read books are usually intelligent …

ⓐ because there are lots of new ideas.

ⓑ because they learn a lot of information from books.

ⓒ because we can read and learn new vocabulary.

ⓓ because they do not need batteries or make any noise.

Refuting Opinions

1. We learn more from books.

2. Watching movies is bad for our health.

3. Reading books is more exciting.

4. It is easier to read a book.

ⓐ This is not true. These days we can watch a movie anywhere using a phone, tablet computer, or music player.

ⓑ Reading books can be unhealthier. This is because we read books for much longer than we watch movies.

ⓒ Not anymore. Movie special effects are amazing.

ⓓ I disagree. When we watch movies, we can learn new vocabulary and learn about different places and cultures.

Opinion Examples

Read the opinions and answer the questions.

 Supporting Opinion    **02** / Unit 1

Books are better than movies because we can read them anywhere. If we want to read a book, that is the only thing that we need. When we watch a movie, we need a television, cell phone, or computer. These machines need electricity to work. Therefore, when there is no power or the battery is dead, it is not possible to watch a movie. In addition, books are sometimes dropped or get wet, but they can still be used. Cell phones that are dropped usually break and stop working.

 **Opposing Opinion**   **03** / Unit 1

Watching a movie is better than reading a book. This is because it is much more exciting. One reason is special effects. When we watch a movie, we can feel that we are in the story or even in another world because of the amazing computer graphics. This is much better than a boring book that is very long. It has no pictures and sometimes smells strange. Furthermore, we can watch a movie with our friends and have fun, but we need to read a book alone, which is boring.

1. Circle the main idea in each opinion.

2. Underline the supporting ideas in each opinion.

3. Can you think of some examples to support the ideas in each opinion?

Discussion Questions

Discuss these questions in groups.

1. After studying all day, do you prefer to read a book or watch a movie?

2. Do you think watching movies stops us from using our imaginations?

3. If you want to learn about something new, is it better to read a book or watch a film about the topic?

4. Is a book with no pictures boring?

5. Which activity is healthier: reading a book or watching a movie?

Let's Debate

Choose one of the statements below and then debate in groups.

1. Children should read books instead of watching movies.

2. Schools should use movies to teach without using books.

3. When there is a book and a movie of the same story, the book is always better.

Unit 2
Eating Insects Instead of Animals

For many people, the idea of eating a bug instead of beef is very strange. However, scientists think we should start eating insects so that we can make sure everyone has enough food to eat.

Think of any insects that you have eaten or heard about. Write down the name of the bug and what it tastes like or what you think it tastes like.

Name of Insect	Taste of Insect

Warm-Up Questions

1. How do you feel about eating bugs every day?

2. Will there be enough food for everybody in the future?

3. Do you want to keep bugs in your house?

Eating Insects Instead of Animals

We usually think that bugs are ugly and cause many problems. But in the future, we may eat insects for breakfast, lunch, and even dinner every day!

Why will we eat insects? First, it will save our environment. Farms with animals need a lot of water, land, and animal food. Animals such as cows and pigs also cause large amounts of greenhouse gases. These gases are making our world warmer. If we eat insects instead of animals, such problems will not occur. Second, bugs are very good for our health. They contain a lot of protein and vitamins, with very little fat. So, people eating insects will be healthier than people eating beef or pork.

The problem is that many people do not want to eat insects. In rich countries, citizens think that bugs are not good foods. People do not change their thinking easily. So, governments cannot make people eat insects. Another problem is that eating bugs can sometimes make us sick. This is because they sometimes contain bad elements. Therefore, people must be very careful when they cook and eat bugs. Finally, many people may still believe that insects are dirty.

Comprehension Check

Answer the questions using information from the reading passage.

1. What are the problems with raising animals?

2. Why is it healthy to eat insects?

3. Why don't many people in rich countries eat insects?

4. Why will governments have difficulty making people eat insects?

5. Why can we be sick if we eat bugs?

Vocabulary Check

Complete each sentence with one of the words below.

environment	government	greenhouse	healthy	protein

1. _____ people do not usually get sick.

2. Many _____ gases come from cars and other vehicles.

3. The _____ does a lot of things for the people.

4. Your body needs _____ to grow well.

5. The _____ can mean land, water, and animals.

Opinion Practice

Practice supporting and refuting the opinions below.

 Supporting Opinions

1. Farming insects is much better for our environment…

2. Eating too much animal meat is bad for our health…

3. Most people do not want to eat bugs…

4. Many families will not stop eating meat…

ⓐ because they think insects are very dirty.

ⓑ because they don't care about the environment.

ⓒ because it means fewer greenhouse gases.

ⓓ because it can make us sick.

 Refuting Opinions

1. Insects will taste really bad.

2. Eating insects is a really great idea.

3. If we farm insects to eat, everyone in the world will have enough food.

4. People won't eat bugs because they are not real food.

ⓐ This is not true. We cannot farm enough insects to give food to all people.

ⓑ This is not true. Many people say that some insects taste really good.

ⓒ Eating insects is strange. Bugs are dirty and cause many problems.

ⓓ People will change their thinking after some time.

Opinion Examples

Read the opinions and answer the questions.

 Supporting Opinion

 **05** / Unit 2

We need to eat insects because it is better for our environment and our bodies. Insect farms will need a lot less land and water. This means we can use the land to grow vegetables and other foods. Therefore, there will be more food for everyone in the world. Also, the bugs that we will eat are healthy for us. So, few people will become sick or fat.

 Opposing Opinion

 **06** / Unit 2

Eating insects is a silly and strange idea. First, people do not want to eat bugs. We live in a good world and we do not want to eat insects. Most people want to eat delicious chicken, beef, or pork. These are real foods that we have enjoyed for a long time. Second, we cannot farm enough insects to feed everyone at the moment. If we stop farming animals today, there will be no meat in the world.

1. Circle the main idea in each opinion.

2. Underline the supporting ideas in each opinion.

3. Can you think of some examples to support the ideas in each opinion?

Discussion Questions

Discuss these questions in groups.

1. How do you feel about eating insect meat if it is 100% safe?

2. Should we stop eating animals if it makes our environment cleaner?

3. Does it matter what the insect meat looks like?

4. Should the government stop the farming of animals?

5. Should we not eat any living animal?

Let's Debate

Choose one of the statements below and then debate in groups.

1. We should eat insect meat instead of animal meat.

2. People living in rich countries do not want to eat insects.

3. The government should give citizens the food they need.

Unit 3
Public Holidays in South Korea

A public holiday is a day when people all over the country do not need to go to school or work. On a public holiday, we can play or rest.

Think about your favorite holiday. Use the box below to make some notes.

Name of the Holiday	
Date of the Holiday	
Reason for the Holiday	
Why I Like This Holiday	

Warm-Up Questions

1. What is your favorite public holiday?

2. What day of the week is best for a public holiday?

3. Do you like public holidays? Why? Why not?

Public Holidays in South Korea

People always hope that public holidays are on weekdays. This is because they can get an extra day off work or school. Many people feel that South Korea needs more public holidays. Then, should the government allow more public holidays?

Some say that South Korea needs more public holidays. First, South Koreans work very long hours and have very short vacations. People in other countries work less and rest more. It is time for South Koreans to rest longer. Second, South Koreans need more time to remember important events in their history. For example, South Korea made the most important law in 1948. The South Korean people should remember such events.

Others disagree. First, on a public holiday, people do not work. This means that fewer things are made and sold. Then, companies may let their workers go. In other words, many people may lose their jobs. Second, on public holidays, people just waste their time. Most people just sleep, watch television, and eat too much. South Koreans should work and study harder without wasting their time.

Comprehension Check

Answer the questions using information from the reading passage.

1. Why do people hope that a public holiday is on a weekday?

2. Why do South Koreans need more public holidays?

3. What kinds of events should people remember from the past?

4. Why is it a problem for South Korea if people do not work on a public holiday?

5. How do people waste their time on a public holiday?

Vocabulary Check

Complete each sentence with one of the words below.

disagree	event	extra	public	weekday

1. You can have a(n) _____ piece of bread.

2. Scientists _____ about the beginning of life.

3. _____ transportation means buses, trains, and airplanes.

4. A(n) _____ means any day of the week except Saturday and Sunday.

5. Her birth is an important _____ for everybody.

Opinion Practice

Practice supporting and refuting the opinions below.

Supporting Opinions

1. More public holidays will help workers to become healthy…

2. Schoolchildren do not need more public holidays…

3. Families will be happier when there are more public holidays…

4. Public holidays are bad for companies…

ⓐ because they need to pay workers for doing nothing.

ⓑ because they can spend time together.

ⓒ because they can rest or exercise.

ⓓ because they have long summer and winter vacations.

Refuting Opinions

1. People waste their time on public holidays.

2. South Korea does not need more public holidays.

3. More public holidays will cost companies too much money.

4. People will remember important events that are celebrated on holidays.

ⓐ That's not correct. Public holidays help workers feel better. As a result, they will work harder after having a public holiday.

ⓑ I disagree. Most people go on trips or do other activities.

ⓒ I disagree. Many public holidays are lost each year because they fall on the weekend.

ⓓ That's not correct. People don't care about why they have a holiday.

Opinion Examples

Read the opinions and answer the questions.

 Supporting Opinion

 **08** / Unit 3

It is important for South Korea to have more public holidays. First, families can spend more time together. Most fathers and many mothers are very busy working. Children are busy studying at schools. Extra holidays will give parents and children the chance to have fun together. In addition, when people have more holidays, they can rest. As a result, workers and students will do even more work after the holiday. This is good for everyone.

 Opposing Opinion

 **09** / Unit 3

Extra public holidays in South Korea are a bad idea. First, they hurt companies and workers. Public holidays mean that people don't work. As a result, companies make less money. Some companies may fail and their workers may lose their jobs. Second, people do nothing on public holidays. It is not healthy to sit and watch television all day. Going to work or school keeps people active.

1. Circle the main idea in each opinion.

2. Underline the supporting ideas in each opinion.

3. Can you think of some examples to support the ideas in each opinion?

Discussion Questions

Discuss these questions in groups.

1. Do you enjoy public holidays?

2. Do South Koreans need more rest?

3. Do you think people care about the reason for a public holiday? Or are they just happy to have a day off from school or work?

4. Will extra public holidays be good or bad for South Korea?

5. Does it matter if people do nothing on a public holiday?

Let's Debate

Choose one of the statements below and then debate in groups.

1. South Koreans need to work much harder.

2. We do not need public holidays at all.

3. People should help others on public holidays.

Unit 4
Four Seasons or One Season?

South Korea has four different seasons. Other countries only have one season all year long. Which is better, one season or four seasons?

Think of the activities you like to do in each season and explain why.

Winter	Activity: Reason:	Activity: Reason:
Spring	Activity: Reason:	Activity: Reason:
Summer	Activity: Reason:	Activity: Reason:
Fall	Activity: Reason:	Activity: Reason:

Warm-Up Questions

1. What is your favorite season?

2. Which season do you like the least?

3. What is the best season for a vacation?

Four Seasons or One Season?

Some countries always have the same season. Other countries, such as Korea, have four different seasons. Which do you think is better?

Some people say that having four seasons is much better. First, we can do many interesting activities. We can go to the beach in the summer. We can go skiing in the winter. In the spring and fall, we can go hiking. Second, we can see nature change from season to season. In the spring and summer, beautiful flowers blossom. In the fall, the leaves of trees change to beautiful orange and red colors.

Other people say that having one season is much better. First, different people like different temperatures. For example, many elderly people like high temperatures. So, they often move to a warm area. Some people like low temperatures and move to a cold area. Second, it is cheaper to live in a place with only one season. This is because you do not have to buy different clothes for each season.

Comprehension Check

Answer the questions using information from the reading passage.

1. How many seasons does Korea have?

2. What can people do in the summer?

3. What happens to the leaves of trees in the fall?

4. Why do many elderly people move to warm areas?

5. Living in an area with one season can be cheaper. Why?

Vocabulary Check

Complete each sentence with one of the words below.

activity	areas	blossom	elderly	temperature

1. The _____ of something means how hot or cold it is.

2. When trees _____, they are full of flowers.

3. _____ people usually need more rest than young people.

4. Urban _____ usually mean cities.

5. Skiing is an exciting _____ for most people.

Opinion Practice

Practice supporting and refuting the opinions below.

 Supporting Opinions

1. Living in an area with one season is easier…

2. Different seasons are much better…

3. Wearing shorts and T-shirts all year is great…

4. Living in a country with four seasons makes our bodies healthier…

ⓐ because we know what the weather will be like every day.

ⓑ because we get used to different weather conditions.

ⓒ because there are many different things to do.

ⓓ because it is cool and comfortable.

Refuting Opinions

1. One season all year is very boring.

2. Having four different seasons is great.

3. There are many different activities to do when there are four seasons.

4. Living in a place that has one season is cheaper.

ⓐ That is not true. Beaches and resorts are too busy, so not all people can enjoy different activities.

ⓑ This is not true. Doing my favorite activity all year is great fun.

ⓒ I am not sure about that. Many places with one season are very hot or cold. It costs a lot of money to pay for the air conditioning or heating.

ⓓ I don't think so. The temperature changes too much. It makes me sick.

Opinion Examples

Read the opinions and answer the questions.

 Supporting Opinion

 **11** / Unit 4

I believe that it is much better to live in a country with four different seasons. Each season, people can do different activities. In the winter, they can do snow sports. In the spring and fall, they can go to the mountains. In the summer, they can go swimming. It is a lot of fun. Also, you can have a stronger body. This is because you can experience hot and cold weather. People living in a place with one season get sick when they go to a country with four different seasons.

 Opposing Opinion

 **12** / Unit 4

It is much better to live in a country with only one season. This is because we know what the weather will be like. People living in a country with four seasons cannot guess the weather conditions. As a result, they may cancel their plans to go hiking or go to the beach. This is because it may rain or become cold. Also, it is healthier to live in a place with the same season. Many people in Korea get sick when the seasons change.

1. Circle the main idea in each opinion.

2. Underline the supporting ideas in each opinion.

3. Can you think of some examples to support the ideas in each opinion?

Discussion Questions

Discuss these questions in groups.

1. Do you think it is healthy to live in a place with one season?

2. Do you think it is boring to have the same season all year round?

3. Do you want to do your favorite activity all year round?

4. How do you feel when a change in weather stops you from doing your favorite activity?

5. Do you want to live in a hot place? Or do you prefer a cold place?

Let's Debate

Choose one of the statements below and then debate in groups.

1. It is more expensive to live in a country with four different seasons.

2. People living in a country with only one season are lazy.

3. People living in a country with four seasons are more active.

Unit 5
Do We Still Need Libraries?

In the past, people went to libraries to find information. However, fewer people are using libraries these days. Do we still need them?

What will make the library in your town a more exciting place for children? Write down your ideas.

1.

2.

3.

4.

Warm-Up Questions

1. How often do you go to a public library?

2. Why do people use libraries?

3. Do you enjoy going to the library?

Do We Still Need Libraries?

Libraries are big buildings with information. People go there to borrow books or find useful information. Students use libraries to find out more about their favorite subjects. These days, however, many people think that we don't need libraries anymore.

They say that the Internet can replace libraries. The Internet helps us find large amounts of information quickly. However, using the library takes much more time. First, we have to travel to the place. Second, we need to find those books we need. Sometimes, they are missing or lost. On the other hand, we can use the Internet 24 hours a day. You can also use it anywhere.

Others disagree. They say that public libraries are great places to study in. In these places, everybody needs to be quiet. That helps people to concentrate on their work. Studying at home is very difficult. This is because there are so many other things to do, such as watching TV or eating a snack. Also, we need libraries because librarians can help us to find useful information. They teach us how to find correct information.

Comprehension Check

Answer the questions using information from the reading passage.

1. What things do people borrow from libraries?

2. Why is it better to find information using the Internet?

3. Why are public libraries great places to study in?

4. Why is it difficult to study at home?

5. Who can help us to find information in the library?

Vocabulary Check

Complete each sentence with one of the words below.

borrow	concentrate	librarian	missing	replacing

1. When you _____ on something, you think carefully about it.

2. E-books are _____ paper books.

3. A _____ works with library books.

4. My family was worried when my dog was _____ .

5. You should ask the owner before you _____ something.

Opinion Practice

Practice supporting and refuting the opinions below.

 Supporting Opinions

1. Libraries are great places to study in…

2. We don't need to go to the library…

3. Library books are not that useful…

4. We need libraries…

ⓐ because they are often old or broken.

ⓑ because they are quiet and have large desks.

ⓒ because some people do not have the Internet.

ⓓ because we can download e-books.

Refuting Opinions

1. Libraries are not needed because Korea has a good Internet service.

2. Libraries are the best places to study in.

3. Nobody uses libraries these days.

4. It is much easier to read information on the Internet.

ⓐ I disagree. Some libraries are very loud, so people cannot concentrate on their work.

ⓑ That is not true. Many people do not like using the Internet.

ⓒ Not really. Reading information on the computer is a difficult thing to do, and it is bad for our eyes.

ⓓ I disagree. People use libraries for many different purposes, such as having a meeting.

Opinion Examples

Read the opinions and answer the questions.

 Supporting Opinion

 **14** / Unit 5

We no longer need public libraries. This is because they are a waste of time and money. If we need information, we can find it by using the Internet. That will take less than a second. However, just traveling to the library takes more time. Sometimes, we cannot find the information we need. Second, many books in public libraries are old. So, they cannot give us new information. This means that libraries are not useful anymore.

 Opposing Opinion

 **15** / Unit 5

Even today, we still need public libraries. First, public libraries are for everyone. Many people do not have enough money to use the Internet or to buy books. By visiting libraries, they can read books and find useful information. Second, people can study easily in public libraries. When students stay at home, they play games or read comic books. However, in libraries, they spend most of their time studying. This is because there are fewer things to do.

1. Circle the main idea in each opinion.

2. Underline the supporting ideas in each opinion.

3. Can you think of some examples to support the ideas in each opinion?

Discussion Questions

Discuss these questions in groups.

1. Will we still have public libraries in 100 years?

2. Are libraries good places to study in?

3. Do you prefer to study at home? Or do you prefer public libraries?

4. Do you usually study with books? Or do you prefer the Internet?

5. Is it OK for students to use library computers to play computer games?

Let's Debate

Choose one of the statements below and then debate in groups.

1. Rich countries do not need public libraries.

2. It is OK for you to talk loudly with your friends in a public library.

3. Every village in South Korea needs a public library.

Unit 6
House or Apartment?

Everybody needs a place to live. Some people want to live in a house, while others prefer apartments. How about you?

What will your dream home look like? Make a sketch of your perfect home and name each room. Tell your partner about your dream home.

Warm-Up Questions

1. Why do many people in South Korea live in an apartment?

2. Do you want to live in a large house?

3. Do you want to live in the tallest apartment in the world?

House or Apartment?

Every day, people buy and sell homes all over the world. Some people buy houses, while others prefer to live in apartments. Most Koreans live in apartments, but some want to live in houses.

Many people say that a house is much better than an apartment. First, houses have much more space than apartments. Most houses have two floors, and some have a basement. As a result, everybody in a family can have privacy. That will help the family members live together. Some houses have gardens. Gardens are great places because families can play and relax there. Second, houses are much quieter than apartments. There are no neighbors making noise. There are no elevators making noise late at night.

Some people think that apartments are much better places to live. First, apartments are very convenient. There are many stores and services close to the apartments. This is really helpful for busy people. These people need to do something quickly. Second, apartments are very safe. They usually have security guards and cameras. As a result, nothing bad will happen to people living in an apartment.

Comprehension Check

Answer the questions using information from the reading passage.

1. Why does a house have more space than an apartment?

2. Why is it good to have a garden?

3. Living in a house is quieter than living in an apartment. Why?

4. Why are apartments convenient?

5. Why are apartments safe?

Vocabulary Check

Complete each sentence with one of the words below.

basements	convenient	neighbor	privacy	security

1. When something is _____, it is useful to you.

2. _____ are usually located below the ground.

3. She needs some _____, so just leave her alone.

4. If we have more _____ cameras, more people will be safe.

5. My next-door _____ is very kind to me.

Opinion Practice

Practice supporting and refuting the opinions below.

Supporting Opinions

1. It is better for children to live in a house… ☐

2. People who live in apartment buildings can have more friends… ☐

3. If you live in a house, you can paint it the color that you like… ☐

4. Living in an apartment is great in the winter… ☐

ⓐ because there are many people living close by.

ⓑ because it is your own home.

ⓒ because you don't need to travel far to buy something.

ⓓ because there is more space to play and have fun.

Refuting Opinions

1. It is much better for a family to live alone in a house. ☐

2. We can have more friends living in an apartment building. ☐

3. Houses have more space to live and play. ☐

4. Apartment buildings have a lot of parking spaces. ☐

ⓐ Not really. Some houses are very small, while some apartments are large.

ⓑ I disagree. A family living alone in a house cannot get help from others.

ⓒ I disagree. Not many apartments have enough parking spaces.

ⓓ I'm not sure about that. Most people living in apartments do not meet their neighbors.

Opinion Examples

Read the opinions and answer the questions.

 Supporting Opinion  **17** / Unit 6

Living in a house is much better than living in an apartment. First, a house is usually much bigger. This is better for children to play and have fun. Also, when children become teenagers, they can have more privacy. Second, the owner of a house is free to decorate the building. House owners can paint their homes any color they choose. They can also build a swimming pool in their gardens.

 Opposing Opinion  **18** / Unit 6

Apartments are much better places to live than houses. First, when you live in an apartment, there are always people to play with or help. There may be a problem with the water or electricity. Then, some people will fix the problem for you. Second, apartment buildings are very convenient. We can do shopping, eat, or get a haircut without going outside. This is very good for busy people.

1. Circle the main idea in each opinion.

2. Underline the supporting ideas in each opinion.

3. Can you think of some examples to support the ideas in each opinion?

Discussion Questions

Discuss these questions in groups.

1. Do you prefer to live in a small house or a small apartment?

2. Is it important to have a garden?

3. Is noise a problem when you live in an apartment?

4. Is it good to have stores and restaurants in an apartment building?

5. Are apartments safer than houses?

Let's Debate

Choose one of the statements below and then debate in groups.

1. Living in a house is healthier than living in an apartment.

2. It is important to have a big house.

3. South Korea needs to build more apartments.

Unit 7
What Should We Learn in School?

Students at school learn subjects like mathematics, English, science, and history. However, do you think they are the best subjects to learn?

 **Think about the subjects you like at school and explain why you like them.**

Subject	Reason Why You Like It

Think of things you want to learn at school and explain why.

Subject You Want to Learn	Reason Why You Want to Learn It

Warm-Up Questions

1. What is the most important subject to learn?

2. Which subject is the least important to learn at school?

3. What life skill do you want to learn?

What Should We Learn in School?

Students study school subjects for many hours each day. They want to score 100% on their tests. Getting a perfect score is great. But are school subjects really useful in real life?

Some people say that most school subjects are a waste of time. First, students will never use them after they get a job. So, they should learn practical skills. They should learn how to cook healthy food. They should learn how to use tools to make something. People need these skills during their lives. Second, learning life skills is much more fun than learning school subjects. If students have fun at school, they will learn more.

Others say that students should learn school subjects. First, most school subjects help students understand the world. For example, history can help the students to understand the past of their country. Science helps them to understand how nature works. Second, school subjects are more difficult to learn. Students can learn practical skills very easily. For example, children can learn how to wash clothes without trouble. So, we don't have to teach these skills at school.

Comprehension Check

Answer the questions using information from the reading passage.

1. Why do most students study many hours each day?

2. Why is it important to learn practical skills?

3. What will happen if students have fun at school?

4. Why should students learn about history?

5. Is it difficult to learn practical skills?

Vocabulary Check

Complete each sentence with one of the words below.

easily	perfect	practical	score	tools

1. If you learn _____ skills, you can use them in real life.

2. Hammers, saws, and shovels are examples of _____.

3. I'm sure we will win the game quite _____.

4. Study harder if you want to get a _____ score.

5. Linda wants to _____ three goals in the game.

Opinion Practice

Practice supporting and refuting the opinions below.

Supporting Opinions

1. We need to know times tables…

2. Students need to learn many different subjects…

3. Learning practical skills is fun…

4. Students need to learn many useful skills…

(a) because companies want workers who have a lot of skills.

(b) because we need to do math every day.

(c) because smart people know a lot of information.

(d) because they are helpful and interesting.

Refuting Opinions

1. Learning about other countries is a waste of time.

2. Students need to learn practical skills to have a better life.

3. Students need to know how to fix things.

4. It is not a good idea to learn about something we will never use.

(a) I don't think so. We can get help from people who can fix things.

(b) I don't think so. If we learn about something, that will help us understand our world better.

(c) I disagree. If we learn about different countries, we can understand our country better.

(d) I disagree. If people are good at school subjects, they will have a better life.

Opinion Examples

Read the opinions and answer the questions.

 Supporting Opinion

 **20** / Unit 7

Schools need to teach students practical skills. First, learning practical skills is much more fun than learning about useless facts. Students can learn how to use tools. They can also learn how to cook. These are skills they will always need. Second, many companies want workers who can solve real problems. Most students know about the past of our country. But not many of them know how to fix a computer. Companies really need people who have practical skills.

 **21** / Unit 7

 **Opposing Opinion**

Students need to learn many different subjects in school such as math and science. First, the world is changing really fast. Students need to learn as much knowledge as possible. Only then can they be successful. Second, learning school subjects can be fun. For example, many students say that they enjoy learning art skills. Some say that they enjoy doing scientific experiments. Enjoying learning is the most important thing in our lives.

1. Circle the main idea in each opinion.

2. Underline the supporting ideas in each opinion.

3. Can you think of some examples to support the ideas in each opinion?

Discussion Questions

Discuss these questions in groups.

1. Is it important to get a perfect score on a test?

2. Should schools teach us how to cook?

3. Should your school allow you to stop learning a subject if you don't like it?

4. Is it important to learn history at school?

5. Is it important to go to a good university?

Let's Debate

Choose one of the statements below and then debate in groups.

1. Schools should teach only practical skills that we need in real life.

2. Schools should allow students to choose between learning school subjects and learning practical skills.

3. Languages are the most important things that students learn at school.

Unit 8
Choosing Where to Go on Vacation

Children don't like vacations because parents choose a place that only adults like. Then, should the parents allow their children to decide where the family will go on vacation?

Think about a vacation that you like. Write the location and explain why it is fun to go to this place.

Location	
Why This Place Is Fun	

Now think about a vacation that you don't like. Write the location and explain why it is not fun to go to this place.

Location	
Why This Place Is Not Fun	

Warm-Up Questions

1. Where do you want to go on vacation?

2. What is the best thing about going on vacation?

3. Do you want to go on vacation with your family? Or do you prefer your friends?

Choosing Where to Go on Vacation

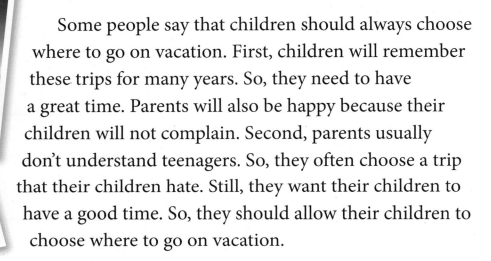

Yumi was excited about going on a beach vacation. Then, her parents decided to go to a mountain on vacation. She was really disappointed. Just like Yumi, many children want to choose the destination for a family vacation.

Some people say that children should always choose where to go on vacation. First, children will remember these trips for many years. So, they need to have a great time. Parents will also be happy because their children will not complain. Second, parents usually don't understand teenagers. So, they often choose a trip that their children hate. Still, they want their children to have a good time. So, they should allow their children to choose where to go on vacation.

Others say that parents need to choose the destination for a family vacation. First, parents think about other family members such as grandparents. They want all the family members to have a good time. Second, children do not know much about the world. They don't understand how big it is. So, they may want to go on a four-day vacation to France. It will disappoint every family member.

Comprehension Check

Answer the questions using information from the reading passage.

1. Why was Yumi disappointed?

2. Why is it important for children to enjoy their vacations?

3. Why do parents often choose a trip that their children hate?

4. Do parents care only about their children?

5. Do children usually understand how big the world is?

Vocabulary Check

Complete each sentence with one of the words below.

complain	disappoint	destination	excited	teenager

1. Your _____ means the place that you are going to.

2. When you are unhappy about something, you _____ about it.

3. A(n) _____ is between 13 and 19 years old.

4. Ashley is a good girl, so she will never _____ us.

5. Many children are _____ about tomorrow's party.

Opinion Practice

Practice supporting and refuting the opinions below.

Supporting Opinions

1. Parents should always choose where to go on vacation…

2. Children should be glad to go on any vacation…

3. A vacation is very special for children…

4. Children will be happier if they choose the vacation destination…

ⓐ because parents don't understand what makes their children happy.

ⓑ because their parents don't have to take them anywhere.

ⓒ because they know more about the world.

ⓓ because they will remember the trip for many years.

Refuting Opinions

1. Children should be happy on a family vacation.

2. A terrible vacation will give children bad feelings for a long time.

3. Children should choose where the family will go on vacation.

4. Most children will never be happy with their vacation. They always want more.

ⓐ I disagree. They will forget most things that happened on the vacation.

ⓑ I disagree. Children just want to do something fun on vacation.

ⓒ I don't think so. Children do not know much about travel destinations.

ⓓ I don't think so. Everyone, not just the children, should be happy on a family vacation.

Opinion Examples

Read the opinions and answer the questions.

 Supporting Opinion

 **23** / Unit 8

Children should decide where the family goes on vacation. First, children need to enjoy their trip. They study very hard in schools. So, they want to have fun for just a few days. They may want to go somewhere for a change. Second, parents don't really understand what their children like. Parents may try their best to choose a good vacation destination for their children. But they often get it wrong. So, it is a better idea to allow children to choose.

 Opposing Opinion

 **24** / Unit 8

Parents should always choose the family vacation destination. First, parents know much more than their children. Children do not know the prices of things. They don't understand that traveling can take a very long time. But their parents can choose a vacation that is not too expensive. They can also choose a destination that is not far away. Second, everybody should be happy on a family vacation. Parents have a very short vacation each year. They need to go on a trip that they like.

1. Circle the main idea in each opinion.

2. Underline the supporting ideas in each opinion.

3. Can you think of some examples to support the ideas in each opinion?

Discussion Questions

Discuss these questions in groups.

1. Do family vacations excite you?

2. Do you think your parents know the things that you like?

3. Who should enjoy the vacation more: children or parents?

4. Should children be thankful that their parents are taking them on vacation?

5. Should parents ask where their children want to go on vacation?

Let's Debate

Choose one of the statements below and then debate in groups.

1. Only children should choose where to go on family vacations.

2. All family members cannot be happy on a family vacation.

3. The best way to decide where to go on vacation is to flip a coin.

Unit 9
Cars that Drive Themselves

Every day, we use cars in many ways. Scientists say that we can make a car that drives itself. Do you think this is a good idea?

 **Imagine that you have a car that can drive itself. What three things do you want to do in the car? You know that you don't need to drive.**

Activity	Reason for the Activity

Warm-Up Questions

1. Do you want to drive a car when you are older?

2. Do you think a computer can safely drive a car?

3. Do we need cars that can drive themselves?

Cars that Drive Themselves

Do you know there are more than one billion cars in the world? Today's cars are much better than those of the past. Still, people need to drive them. A driverless car may be a good thing for all of us.

Some people say that we need to make driverless cars. First, today's cars are still very dangerous. Each year, over one million people die in traffic accidents. This is because people make too many mistakes. They may get tired, but computers do not. So, if computers drive cars, the roads will be much safer. Second, in driverless cars, people can do other activities. For example, businesspeople can do their work. Parents can take care of their children. People don't have to waste time driving their cars.

Other people say that we should not make driverless cars. First, computers make errors too. They are not perfect. So, they sometimes stop working. If the computer in a driverless car stops working, it can cause a very big accident. Second, most people enjoy driving their cars. For many people, driving their cars means that they can relax without worrying about their work. Some people may want to drive their cars to beautiful places.

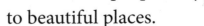

Comprehension Check

Answer the questions using information from the reading passage.

1. How many cars are there in the world?

2. How many people die in traffic accidents each year?

3. Why do traffic accidents happen?

4. What things can people do in a driverless car?

5. What do many people think about driving their cars?

Vocabulary Check

Complete each sentence with one of the words below.

| accident | dangerous | error | relax | tired |

1. When you make a(n) _____, you make a mistake.

2. When you _____, you rest or do something that you enjoy.

3. Linda was too _____ to do her homework.

4. Sadly, many people died in the traffic _____.

5. Many people say that the town is a _____ place to live.

Opinion Practice

Practice supporting and refuting the opinions below.

 Supporting Opinions

1. Driverless cars will be useful for everyone…

2. People do not need to drive cars…

3. People like to drive…

4. Most people do not want driverless cars…

ⓐ because they do not believe that computers are perfect.

ⓑ because many people, such as young children, can use them.

ⓒ because they enjoy controlling their cars themselves.

ⓓ because computers are much safer than people.

 Refuting Opinions

1. Driverless cars will help everyone.

2. Driverless cars will save travel time.

3. People enjoy driving.

4. Everyone will have a driverless car in the future.

ⓐ I don't think so. It will take a lot of time for us to develop driverless cars.

ⓑ I don't think so. For example, driverless cars will make taxi drivers lose their jobs.

ⓒ I disagree. Most people drive their cars because they have to.

ⓓ I disagree. If people can use driverless cars, there will be more cars on the road.

Opinion Examples

Read the opinions and answer the questions.

 Supporting Opinion

 **26** / Unit 9

Driverless cars will make the world a better place. First, everybody can use the driverless car. Children can travel to school without their parents. Disabled people can travel alone quite easily. Second, driverless cars will be very safe. People make mistakes. This causes accidents. Driverless cars will be safer because computers can do things better than people.

 Opposing Opinion

 **27** / Unit 9

Driverless cars are not better than traditional cars. First, most people enjoy driving their cars. People love the freedom to go anywhere in their cars. They can control the speed of their car. People have driven cars for more than 100 years. Driving is part of our lives. Second, the technology for driverless cars is very expensive. Companies are still doing experiments to test the cars. Many of these experiments fail because the driverless cars do not work well.

1. Circle the main idea in each opinion.

2. Underline the supporting ideas in each opinion.

3. Can you think of some examples to support the ideas in each opinion?

Discussion Questions

Discuss these questions in groups.

1. Why do you think traffic accidents happen?

2. Do you think people like driving their cars?

3. Do you think computers can do things better than people?

4. Do you want to use a driverless car on your own?

5. Should we develop driverless cars?

Let's Debate

Choose one of the statements below and then debate in groups.

1. Driverless cars will be faster than traditional cars.

2. People are better drivers than computers.

3. We do not need driverless cars.

Unit 10
Children Doing Chores

In Korea, adults spend a lot of time cleaning their houses. Should they make their children do such chores?

Look at the chores below. Rank them from best to worst (1 is best, 5 is worst). Then explain why you have chosen that order.

taking out the trash	cleaning the bathroom	going shopping
doing the laundry	cleaning the floor	

1.

2.

3.

4.

5.

Warm-Up Questions

1. Is it important for children to do the chores at home?

2. Who does the chores in your home?

3. Is it fun to do housework?

DC1-10 MP3

Children Doing Chores

Nobody enjoys doing chores. But somebody should do them. If we don't do housework, our homes will be very dirty. In many countries, children start doing the chores at a young age. But Korean children do not usually do the chores. Should this change?

Some people say that Korean children should do chores. First, it will teach them life skills. All adults need to know how to do the laundry. They also need to know how to cook. If children practice these skills at a young age, they will become adults with practical skills. Second, doing the chores is good exercise. Sadly, Korean children spend too much time sitting down. Doing housework will allow them to do more exercise. It will make the children healthier.

Other people say that Korean children should not do chores. First, Korean children need to study really hard. They have to get good grades to have a better life. If they do housework, they do not study. This can be a problem. Second, doing chores can be dangerous. Cooking needs knives and fire. Cleaning needs chemicals. These things can injure children.

Comprehension Check

Answer the questions using information from the reading passage.

1. What will happen if we don't do chores?

2. Why do children need to learn life skills?

3. How can doing chores improve children's health?

4. Why do some people think Korean children should focus on studying?

5. Why can chores be dangerous?

Vocabulary Check

Complete each sentence with one of the words below.

adult	change	chemicals	injures	laundry

1. When something _____ you, it hurts you.

2. When you do the _____, you wash dirty clothes and towels.

3. This terrible situation should _____.

4. A(n) _____ is a fully-grown person.

5. Some _____, such as oil, are made naturally.

Opinion Practice

Practice supporting and refuting the opinions below.

Supporting Opinions

1. Young children enjoy chores…

2. Children should not do chores…

3. Children should study without doing chores…

4. Children doing housework are helpful…

ⓐ because they need to have fun before they become adults.

ⓑ because their parents have fewer chores to do at home.

ⓒ because they like to feel that they are doing real work.

ⓓ because schoolwork is more important.

Refuting Opinions

1. Children help their parents by doing chores.

2. Children in Korea don't have enough free time to do chores.

3. Children who do chores learn about teamwork.

4. Children should play outside without doing housework.

ⓐ I don't think so. Playing sports is a better way to learn about teamwork.

ⓑ I don't think so. Children usually do the chores badly, so their parents need to do them again.

ⓒ I disagree. Playing outside is dangerous in many areas. Doing chores is a good way to get exercise.

ⓓ I disagree. Doing chores doesn't take a long time.

Opinion Examples

Read the opinions and answer the questions.

 Supporting Opinion

Children need to do chores. First, children can learn important skills such as cleaning and cooking. They can also learn about teamwork and helping others. All these skills can help a child to become a hard-working person. People who work hard usually have a better life. Second, parents will have more free time if their children help them with the housework. Then, the parents will have less stress. As a result, they may want to do fun activities with their children.

 Opposing Opinion

Korean children should not do housework. First, students should use their free time to play outside with friends. Korean children spend too much time indoors. If they do the chores at home, they use dangerous chemicals. It is more important for the children to get fresh air. Second, children usually don't do the chores correctly. Most children hate doing housework. So they try to finish as quickly as possible. As a result, parents still need to do all the chores at home.

1. Circle the main idea in each opinion.

2. Underline the supporting ideas in each opinion.

3. Can you think of some examples to support the ideas in each opinion?

Discussion Questions

Discuss these questions in groups.

1. Do you think doing chores is dangerous?

2. Do you think it is important to know how to cook?

3. Can chores help children to be healthier?

4. Do you think doing chores is more important than studying school subjects?

5. How often should children do the chores each week?

Let's Debate

Choose one of the statements below and then debate in groups.

1. Korean parents should make their children do the chores at home.

2. Children should do chores every day.

3. Children should be paid for doing the chores.

Unit 11
Students Should Have Part-Time Jobs

Almost every adult has a job. But most students do not have jobs. Maybe they need to have part-time jobs.

Think about a part-time job that you want to have. Then answer the following questions.

Job Name	
How many hours do you want to work each week?	
Why do you want this job?	
What skills do you want to learn?	

Warm-Up Questions

1. Do you have a part-time job? What do you do?

2. When should students start doing part-time jobs?

3. Should students be paid less than adults?

DC1-11
MP3

Students Should Have Part-Time Jobs

Korean students learn many subjects. But they don't have part-time jobs. In many countries, however, students start doing part-time work when they are thirteen. Should Korean students get part-time jobs when they are teenagers?

Some people say that Korean students should have part-time jobs. First, they can learn skills that they cannot learn in school. For example, they may learn how to open or close a store. They may learn to look after the money. They may learn how to treat customers well. Second, if students have part-time jobs, they can learn to take care of themselves. They learn to be on time at work. They learn to be responsible for their behavior.

Other people say that Korean students should not have part-time jobs. First, it is very difficult to study and work at the same time. If Korean students do both things, they may get lower grades. That will stop students from being successful in the future. Second, having part-time jobs is not good for students' health. Working and studying will make students very tired. When they are tired, they may get sick easily.

Comprehension Check

Answer the questions using information from the reading passage.

1. When do students start doing part-time work in many countries?

2. What skills can students learn by doing part-time work?

3. How can students with part-time jobs learn to take care of themselves?

4. Why is it a problem if students get lower grades?

5. Why is it a problem if students are tired because of studying and working?

Vocabulary Check

Complete each sentence with one of the words below.

behavior	customers	part-time	responsible	successful

1. When you are _____ for a mistake, people blame you for it.

2. Your _____ means the things you do.

3. When you have a _____ job, you work for only part of each day.

4. _____ people usually make a lot of money.

5. Her store serves about one hundred _____ each day.

Opinion Practice

Practice supporting and refuting the opinions below.

Supporting Opinions

1. Students will have no free time if they study and work…

2. Students should focus on their studies…

3. Students can have fun by doing a part-time job…

4. It is good for teenagers to earn money by doing part-time jobs…

ⓐ because they can buy the things that they want.

ⓑ because they need to get good grades.

ⓒ because they will have too many things to do.

ⓓ because they can meet a lot of people.

Refuting Opinions

1. Students can learn many useful skills by doing part-time jobs.

2. Teenagers enjoy working part-time.

3. Most Korean parents don't want their children to work.

4. It is not safe for teenagers to do part-time work.

ⓐ That is not true. Many rules protect all workers, including teenagers.

ⓑ I disagree. Part-time jobs, such as working in a store, do not teach many useful skills.

ⓒ That is not true. Most teenagers dislike their boring part-time jobs.

ⓓ I disagree. Many parents think both studying and working are important.

Opinion Examples

Read the opinions and answer the questions.

 Supporting Opinion

 32 / Unit 11

Students should have part-time jobs. First, they can have fun by doing their job. This is because students can often work with their friends. So, they can forget about their studies for a few hours each week. As a result, they will have less stress. Second, teenagers can earn their own money. This is important because students want to buy many things. If students work, they can buy some of the things themselves. As a result, they will not ask their parents for money.

 Opposing Opinion

 33 / Unit 11

It is a bad idea for students to have part-time jobs. First, if students have part-time jobs, they cannot focus on their schoolwork. In Korea, it is important for students to get good grades. This is because they want to go to good schools and universities. Second, students with part-time jobs will have no free time at all. Korean teenagers are already busy learning school subjects. If they work too, they will not have any time to do something fun.

1. Circle the main idea in each opinion.

2. Underline the supporting ideas in each opinion.

3. Can you think of some examples to support the ideas in each opinion?

Discussion Questions

Discuss these questions in groups.

1. Do you think that thirteen is a good age to start doing part-time work?

2. Is it important for teenagers to earn their own money? Why?

3. Is it difficult to study and work at the same time?

4. How many hours should students work each week?

5. Will companies hire workers with great grades?

Let's Debate

Choose one of the statements below and then debate in groups.

1. All elementary school students should have part-time jobs.

2. Teenagers learn more skills by doing part-time work than by going to school.

3. We should allow students to work for three hours each day.

Unit 12
Money Is the Best Gift

Our family and friends give us gifts at special times. Sometimes, however, they give us gifts that we don't like. If they just give us money, we may not be disappointed.

Think of presents that somebody gave you. Did you like them? If not, explain why you were disappointed.

The Gift that Somebody Gave You	The Reason(s) You Did Not Like It

Warm-Up Questions

1. Do you like to give gifts to people?

2. What did you do with a gift that you didn't like?

3. Do you know what your best friend wants to receive as a gift?

Money Is the Best Gift

We give gifts to other people to celebrate special events, such as birthdays. But we can't be sure if they will like our presents for them. Giving money as a gift may solve this problem.

Some people say that money is a great gift. First, money can be used for so many things. With money, we can buy something in a store or eat at a nice restaurant. We can also save the money in our bank. Second, giving money as a gift saves time. We don't have to worry about finding the perfect present. We often don't know what other people want to receive as a gift. If we just give them money, we don't have to worry at all.

Other people say that money is not a great gift. First, we give presents to others at special times. So, the presents should be special, too. It is important for us to make efforts to find special presents for others. It is very lazy to give money as a gift. Second, receiving money as a gift is not special at all. We are often surprised at special gifts. As a result, we feel special. If we receive money as a gift, we won't feel special.

Comprehension Check

Answer the questions using information from the reading passage.

1. Why do people give gifts to others?

2. What can we do by using money?

3. Why does it save time to give money as a gift?

4. Why should the gifts we give be special?

5. When do we feel special?

Vocabulary Check

Complete each sentence with one of the words below.

celebrate	effort	event	save	special

1. A(n) _____ means something that happens, usually something unusual.

2. When you make a(n) _____ , you try to do something.

3. You can _____ energy if you turn off the lights.

4. When you _____ a holiday, you do something interesting on that day.

5. They are planning to do something _____ for Christmas.

Opinion Practice

Practice supporting and refuting the opinions below.

 Supporting Opinions

1. Giving money as a gift can save a lot of time…

2. People should give money as a gift…

3. It is not a good idea to give money instead of a gift to children…

4. Gifts are more special than money…

ⓐ because they will waste the cash on snacks or computer games.

ⓑ because we don't have to go shopping for gifts.

ⓒ because there will be no more terrible presents.

ⓓ because we can keep the gifts for many years.

Refuting Opinions

1. Giving money as a gift is not special.

2. Giving money as a gift does not cause stress.

3. We can keep gifts for many years.

4. Nobody will be unhappy if they receive money as a gift.

ⓐ That is not true. Gifts often break or become old.

ⓑ I disagree. Most people prefer special gifts to money.

ⓒ That is not true. People worry about how much money they should give.

ⓓ I disagree. Money is special because we can do so many things with it.

Opinion Examples

Read the opinions and answer the questions.

 Supporting Opinion

 **35** / Unit 12

Money is the best gift that we can give. First, if we receive money from our family and friends, we won't be unhappy. If we receive a terrible gift, we feel unhappy. Giving money as a gift can solve this problem. Second, giving money as a gift does not cause stress. We don't have to spend a lot of time shopping for someone. We don't have to worry about whether the receiver will be happy with the gift we buy.

 Opposing Opinion

 **36** / Unit 12

Giving a gift is much better than giving money. First, presents are for special events. So, we should think carefully about what to buy. When the person receives the gift, he or she will think it is special. This is because we take the time to buy the gift. Second, giving money to children is a bad idea. Children love to spend money very quickly. As a result, most children will spend the money on things that they don't need. Or they will spend the money on junk foods that are bad for their health.

1. Circle the main idea in each opinion.

2. Underline the supporting ideas in each opinion.

3. Can you think of some examples to support the ideas in each opinion?

Discussion Questions

Discuss these questions in groups.

1. Do you feel happy when a person gives you money?

2. Do you think it is easy to give money as a gift?

3. Is it difficult to buy a gift for other people?

4. Do you think it is lazy to give money as a gift?

5. What will happen if people give each other money as gifts?

 Let's Debate

Choose one of the statements below and then debate in groups.

1. Money is the worst gift.

2. We should give presents to each other instead of giving money.

3. A gift that we make is more special than a gift from a store.

Unit 13
Teacher or No Teacher?

Many students say that they learn better from teachers than from computers. Others disagree. Do you believe computers should replace teachers?

 **Look at the list of subjects below. Do you want to learn the subject with a teacher? Or do you prefer to learn from computers?**

Subject	Teachers or Computers	Reasons
English		
History		
Mathematics		
Science		

Warm-Up Questions

1. Why do we have teachers?

2. Do you want to learn school subjects from computers?

3. Do you believe that computers can replace teachers?

Teacher or No Teacher?

Teachers have a lot of knowledge. They can help their students to learn a lot of different subjects. However, some people want to replace teachers with computers. Are they correct?

Many people believe that we do not need teachers these days. First, students can find the answer to any question by using computers and the Internet. Teachers will never know all the answers or the latest information. Second, students can learn better by using computers and the Internet. They can study fast or slow. They can focus on particular learning points. They can communicate with other students by using the Internet.

Other people say that computers and the Internet cannot replace teachers. First, teachers can help students learn more. This is because they can explain information in many different ways. They can check whether their students understand certain points. Computers cannot do this. Second, teachers make sure that their students are really studying in class. If there are no teachers in class, the students will misbehave or play computer games.

Comprehension Check

Answer the questions using information from the reading passage.

1. Why can teachers help their students learn a lot of subjects?

2. Why does the Internet help students to learn?

3. Explain why students can learn better by using computers.

4. Why can students learn more with teachers?

5. What will students do when there are no teachers in class?

Vocabulary Check

Complete each sentence with one of the words below.

communicate	focus	latest	particular	replaces

1. A _____ thing is the thing that you are talking about.

2. If a pen _____ a pencil, the pen is used instead of the pencil.

3. Yumi should _____ more on her studies.

4. We can _____ with other people by using the Internet.

5. The _____ information is the newest information.

Opinion Practice

Practice supporting and refuting the opinions below.

 Supporting Opinions

1. Students will study less when there is no teacher… ☐

2. Students can learn more by using computers… ☐

3. We need teachers in the classroom… ☐

4. It is cheaper to use only computers to learn… ☐

ⓐ because teachers are more expensive.

ⓑ because they can teach themselves how to do something.

ⓒ because there is nobody to stop them from playing.

ⓓ because they do many important jobs in the classroom.

 Refuting Opinions

1. Students can use the Internet to find all the information that they need. ☐

2. Students can learn at their own speed when they learn from computers. ☐

3. We need teachers because they help us to do our best. ☐

4. Teachers make sure that students do their work. ☐

ⓐ I disagree. Many students don't want to go to school because their teachers are not nice people.

ⓑ I disagree. There is so much incorrect information on the Internet.

ⓒ I don't think so. Many students do not know how to use computers in a helpful way.

ⓓ I don't think so. Teachers cannot control everyone because there are too many students in the classroom.

Opinion Examples

Read the opinions and answer the questions.

 Supporting Opinion

 **38** / Unit 13

Students should learn from computers without learning from teachers. First, students can learn much more by using computers and the Internet. They can find all the information they need on the Internet. Second, students don't have to worry about teachers. Some teachers give their students too much homework. Others are not kind to their students. This will not be a problem if students learn from computers. As a result, they will learn more because they have less stress.

 **Opposing Opinion**

39 / Unit 13

Students always need teachers to help them learn. First, teachers make sure that students do their work and learn. If there is no teacher in the class, students will sleep or play computer games. As a result, the students who want to study cannot focus on their studies. Second, we need teachers because they do many things for students. Teachers help their students to understand the importance of working with other people. They also encourage them to be polite. These things are very important.

1. Circle the main idea in each opinion.

2. Underline the supporting ideas in each opinion.

3. Can you think of some examples to support the ideas in each opinion?

Discussion Questions

Discuss these questions in groups.

1. Is it easy to find the answers to schoolwork on the Internet?

2. If you don't understand a question, will you use the Internet to understand it better?

3. Do you think your classmates will study if there are no teachers in the classroom?

4. Are there any lessons that always need a teacher?

5. If we don't need teachers, will we still need schools in the future?

Let's Debate

Choose one of the statements below and then debate in groups.

1. We don't need teachers anymore in the classroom.

2. Students can learn more by using computers.

3. Students will have less stress if they learn from computers.

Unit 14
Using Public Transportation

Many people use their cars to travel to work or the supermarket. However, it will be much better if everyone uses public transportation such as buses, trains, and subways.

Look at the destinations in the table below. Decide on the best way to get there from your home. Explain why you have made each choice.

Destination	Type of Transportation	Reasons
City Hall, at 9 a.m.		
Busan, just before Chuseok.		
Your friend's place, at night.		
City Library, in the morning.		

Warm-Up Questions

1. Do you like to use public transportation?

2. Have you ever been stuck in a traffic jam? What was it like?

3. What is your favorite way to travel? Why?

Using Public Transportation

When we want to go somewhere, we have two different choices. We can drive our cars. Or we can use public transportation. Many scientists believe that we should choose public transportation.

These scientists say that we need to use public transportation without using our cars. First, it is much better for the environment. Buses and trains can carry a lot of people. But they do not cause much pollution. However, cars cannot carry many people. They also cause much pollution. Second, the roads will be less busy if everybody uses public transportation. Then, there will be fewer traffic jams. As a result, people can travel to their destinations much faster.

Other people say that using cars is better than using public transportation. First, using a car is much more convenient. If a family uses their car to travel, they can travel at any time. They don't need to stop to pick up other people. Second, traveling by car is healthier. A lot of people get sick when they use public transportation. This is because it is often too crowded. There are sometimes people who cough in front of others.

Comprehension Check

Answer the questions using information from the reading passage.

1. How many choices do we have when we want to go somewhere?

2. Why is public transportation better for the environment?

3. Why will there be fewer traffic jams if more people use public transportation?

4. Why is it more convenient to drive a car?

5. Why do a lot of people get sick on public transportation?

Vocabulary Check

Complete each sentence with one of the words below.

convenient	cough	crowded	jam	pollution

1. When you are stuck in a traffic _____, your car can only move very slowly.

2. When a room is _____, it is full of people or things.

3. Air _____ is bad for our health.

4. 2:00 p.m. is _____ for the engineer.

5. When you _____, you push air out of your throat suddenly.

Opinion Practice

Practice supporting and refuting the opinions below.

 **Supporting Opinions**

1. Public transportation is cheaper… ☐

2. It is better for a family with children to travel by car… ☐

3. Public transportation is much faster… ☐

4. Traveling by car is quicker… ☐

ⓐ because it is difficult to transfer with children at busy bus stations.

ⓑ because the passenger does not have to pay for fuel or other costs.

ⓒ because the driver can go directly to his or her destination.

ⓓ because there are no traffic jams on the subway.

 Refuting Opinions

1. It is easier for a family to travel by car. ☐

2. Traveling by car is much faster because there are no stations to stop at. ☐

3. Using public transportation is cheaper than driving a car. ☐

4. Public transportation is better for the environment. ☐

ⓐ It is not cheaper if parents and children are traveling together. It is expensive.

ⓑ I disagree. It is often very difficult to drive and control children at the same time.

ⓒ I don't think so. Cars are often stuck in traffic jams.

ⓓ I don't think so. Old buses and trains cause a lot of pollution.

Opinion Examples

Read the opinions and answer the questions.

 Supporting Opinion

 **41** / Unit 14

When we travel somewhere, it is always better to use public transportation. First, it is usually much cheaper. This is because passengers only need to pay a small fee. They don't have to pay for fuel or other costs. Second, public transportation is better for the environment. Many buses use green energy and clean fuels. Most cars use gasoline. It makes the air dirty. If everybody uses public transportation more, the world will be cleaner.

 Opposing Opinion

 **42** / Unit 14

Traveling by car is much better than using public transportation. First, driving cars is fast. This is because drivers can travel directly to their destinations. They don't have to worry about missing the bus or train. Second, it is easier for families to travel by car. Everybody has a seat. Young children can play happily. They do not bother other passengers. Also, drivers have less stress if their families have a lot of baggage. They don't have to carry it around.

1. Circle the main idea in each opinion.

2. Underline the supporting ideas in each opinion.

3. Can you think of some examples to support the ideas in each opinion?

Discussion Questions

Discuss these questions in groups.

1. Is public transportation really better for the environment?

2. Will you prefer to use a subway if it is twice as fast as a car?

3. Does your family prefer to travel by car? Why?

4. What can the government do to make public transportation more popular?

5. Should there be more buses and trains late at night?

Choose one of the statements below and then debate in groups.

1. Everyone must travel on public transportation.

2. Public transportation should be free.

3. Public transportation will never replace cars.

Unit 15
I Want to Be Famous!

We can see famous people in magazines, on the Internet, and on television. They have great jobs and look so happy. So, I want to be famous, too!

Imagine that you are a famous person. Look at the table below and answer the questions.

Questions	Answer and Reasons
Where do you live?	
Where do you go on vacation?	
What foods do you usually eat?	
What hobbies do you have?	

Warm-Up Questions

1. What famous person do you want to meet? Why?

2. What is the best thing about being famous?

3. Why do you want to be famous?

I Want to Be Famous!

A lot of people want to be famous. They believe that famous people have an amazing life. Then, do you want to be famous too?

Some people say that being famous is fantastic. First, famous people can become rich. Many famous people get paid a lot of money to do their jobs. For example, famous singers and actors are paid millions of dollars each year. Second, famous people can do many interesting things. They can travel all over the world. They can also meet powerful people like presidents. In addition, they can go to special events such as fashion shows and sports finals.

Other people say that being famous has many disadvantages. First, no privacy is a big problem. Fans and photographers always take pictures of famous people. This means that somebody will always be watching famous people. This is annoying. Second, people become jealous of famous people. As a result, many people write horrible things about them on the Internet. These people can also start rumors. This can make a famous person's life difficult and unhappy.

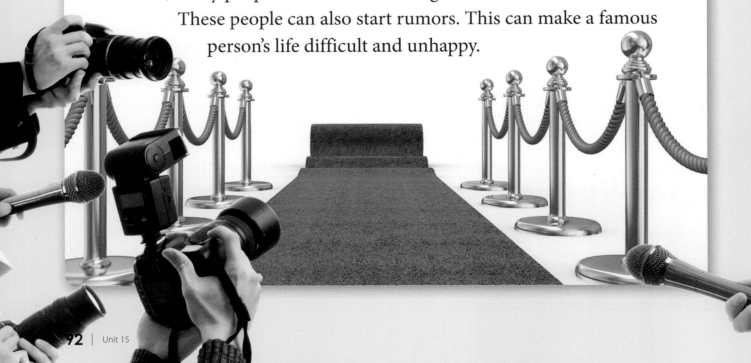

Comprehension Check

Answer the questions using information from the reading passage.

1. Why do many people want to be famous?

2. Why are many famous people rich?

3. What interesting things can famous people do?

4. Why do famous people have no privacy?

5. Why do many people write horrible things about famous people on the Internet?

Vocabulary Check

Complete each sentence with one of the words below.

annoying	disadvantage	fantastic	jealous	powerful

1. If you are _____ of your friend's toy, you are unhappy because he or she has the toy.

2. This beautiful house is really _____!

3. _____ people like presidents can do a lot of things.

4. If something is _____, it makes you a little angry.

5. A(n) _____ is something that causes problems.

Opinion Practice

Practice supporting and refuting the opinions below.

Supporting Opinions

1. Famous people are given a lot of free things by companies…

2. Famous people can help to make changes in society…

3. Famous people cannot live a usual life…

4. Famous people don't have many friends…

ⓐ because their fans will do what they ask them.

ⓑ because they worry about their friends telling other people their secrets.

ⓒ because they think they can sell more if a famous person uses their products.

ⓓ because fans always ask them for their autographs and photos.

Refuting Opinions

1. A famous person has a great life.

2. Famous people are usually rich.

3. People say bad things about famous people.

4. Fans will always ask for photographs and autographs.

ⓐ I don't think so. Few people start bad rumors about famous people.

ⓑ I don't think so. Most famous people cannot make much money. Many singers and actors need to pay money to their management company.

ⓒ I disagree. There are many fans that are just happy to see their stars.

ⓓ I disagree. The popularity of a famous person does not last long.

Opinion Examples

Read the opinions and answer the questions.

 Supporting Opinion

Being a famous person is fantastic. First, famous people do not need to pay for things. This is because companies give them their products for free. In fact, famous people usually get free items before other people can buy them. Second, famous people can make our world a better place to live. This is because their fans listen to what they say. They trust the famous people. As a result, famous people can stop bad things from happening in our world.

 **Opposing Opinion**

It is not good to be a famous person. First, most famous people are famous only for a short time. Not many of them become rich. When they are no longer famous, these people feel sad and unhappy. Second, famous people don't have many friends and feel lonely. This is because famous people cannot trust other people easily. They worry that their friends may tell other people about their secrets. This is a sad life.

1. Circle the main idea in each opinion.

2. Underline the supporting ideas in each opinion.

3. Can you think of some examples to support the ideas in each opinion?

Discussion Questions

Discuss these questions in groups.

1. Do you still want to be famous if you cannot become rich?

2. Do you want to advertise a product that you do not like?

3. How will you feel if people keep asking you for your autographs?

4. If your best friend becomes famous, will you become jealous of him or her?

5. Do you think famous people are making our world a better place?

Let's Debate

Choose one of the statements below and then debate in groups.

1. It is great to be a famous person.

2. All famous people are talented.

3. Famous people should be allowed to protect their privacy.

Unit 16
Spend or Save?

Sometimes, children get money from their parents for doing chores. What should they do with the money? Should they spend it or save it?

Look at the different amounts of money in the table below. Decide if you will save or spend the cash. Explain your reasons. Also, if you decide to spend the money, what will you buy?

Amount of Money	Save the Money	Spend the Money
₩ 500		
₩ 1,000		
₩ 10,000		
₩ 100,000		

Warm-Up Questions

1. Do you like to spend your money?

2. What things do you like to buy?

3. Do your parents stop you from spending your money?

Spend or Save?

Many children feel happy when they get money from their parents. Do they need to keep the money in their pockets? Or do they need to spend it? What do you think?

Some people say that children should spend their money. First, it feels great to buy things that we want. Most children in Korea study very hard and don't have much fun. If they buy something that they want, they will feel happy. Second, children need to learn about wasting money. They need to understand how it feels to buy something useless. This is an important lesson to learn. If children learn this lesson, they will not waste their money when they are older.

Other people say that children should save their money. First, young children need to learn to save money. This is because they should learn to keep money for their future. People who don't know how to save become poor. Second, children can have a lot of money by saving their money. When they save money in a bank, it gives them more money. As a result, if they keep saving, they can become quite rich.

Comprehension Check

Answer the questions using information from the reading passage.

1. When do many children feel happy?

2. How do students feel when they buy something that they want?

3. Why is it important for children to waste money when they are young?

4. Why should children learn to save when they are young?

5. Saving money in the bank is a great idea. Why?

Vocabulary Check

Complete each sentence with one of the words below.

bank	lessons	poor	useless	waste

1. _____ people have very little money.

2. It is not a good idea to _____ your money on that snack.

3. We can borrow money from the _____.

4. We can learn many _____ from our experiences.

5. _____ things are not useful at all.

Opinion Practice

Practice supporting and refuting the opinions below.

Supporting Opinions

1. Children feel happy when they spend their money…

2. It is a good idea for children to save money…

3. Spending money helps children learn about using their money…

4. Saving money means that children don't waste their money…

- ⓐ because they will have money for the future.
- ⓑ because they can buy exciting things that they enjoy.
- ⓒ because they do not buy things that they do not need.
- ⓓ because they understand how much things cost.

Refuting Opinions

1. If children save all their money, they will not waste it.

2. Children should save their money in banks because they give them more money.

3. It is such a waste for children to spend their money on silly things.

4. Children feel happy when they buy things that they really want.

- ⓐ I disagree. Children need to learn about wasting money. Then they will not waste much money when they are adults.
- ⓑ I disagree. Children get bored with things very easily. They always want something new.
- ⓒ I don't think so. Children who always save money do not learn about what it means to waste money.
- ⓓ I don't think so. Banks do not usually give children much money.

Opinion Examples

Read the opinions and answer the questions.

 Supporting Opinion

 **47** / Unit 16

It is important for children to spend their money. First, they can buy things that they like. Children can have fun by buying exciting toys, interesting magazines, or delicious foods. These things make them very happy. Second, children who spend their money learn not to waste it. When children buy something silly, they understand what it means to waste money. As a result, they don't waste money when they are older.

 Opposing Opinion

 **48** / Unit 16

If children have money, they must save it. First, children need to save money for the future. When they are older, they will need money for many different things such as university. Children who do not save will not have enough money when they are adults. Second, children will learn that they cannot buy everything that they want. Children who save will think carefully about what they really need to buy. As a result, they will not waste their money on things they do not need.

1. Circle the main idea in each opinion.

2. Underline the supporting ideas in each opinion.

3. Can you think of some examples to support the ideas in each opinion?

Discussion Questions

Discuss these questions in groups.

1. If you save money, where is the best place to keep it?

2. Do you feel good after spending your money?

3. Is it a problem if children waste their money?

4. What are some things children should buy with their money?

5. Should parents make their children save money?

  Let's Debate

Choose one of the statements below and then debate in groups.

1. It is better for children to spend their money.

2. Children who save money will be happier in the future.

3. Parents should decide if their children should spend or save their money.